THE LIVE FIRST MOVEMENT PRESENTS:

LIVE! 5 Steps to Being More Free Spirited

Tamika Lang

Copyright © 2021 Tamika Lang
All rights reserved.
ISBN: 9798782118297

TABLE OF CONTENTS

Intro 1

Chapter 1: Define You for You 5
    Journal time 10

Chapter 2: Care Less so You Can Do and Be More 13
    Journal time 18

Chapter 3: Remove Consequential Mentality 21
    Journal time 25

Chapter 4: Forgive 29
    Journal Time 33

Chapter 5: Start and Stay the Course 39
    Journal Time 42

Outro 49

INTRO

I am soooo excited to finally sit down and write this book! It's been years in the making, and now it's time! After 2020 kicked all of our asses and 2021 decided to try to one-up its predecessor, this book has been nagging at my soul and begging to be freed! So here we go!

For many years I battled anxiety and depression. I was just like so many people who struggled to figure out my place in the world. When I was up, I was up…but man, when I was down I was beyond down. There were suicide attempts, hospitalizations, medications - you name it! In 2001 I found myself at the first bottom I had ever experienced. I was staring at myself in a mirror and asked over and over, "Who are you? Who do you want to be?" I felt empty and unfulfilled, chasing dreams that I never felt connected to. Living from one day to the next based on who I needed to be for my son, my family - thinking I had saved enough of myself for myself, only to realize I barely knew who that self was.

That same year, India Arie released her first album, *Acoustic Soul*. There is a song on the album called *Beautiful*. When I tell you every single word of that song inspired me. It shook my soul. Sometimes I'd hear it and big, ugly, snot-faced cry...other times I'd hear it and feel peace and purposed. Both responses established that song as necessary to the soundtrack of my life. The resonation of the lyrics gave me the courage to define what beautiful in this world could be for me, and it was the first time I had ever heard anyone express with sincerity that they needed to choose themselves so they could be great for those around them...at least that's how I interpreted it. So I put the song on repeat and took the first leap of faith on the path to freeing my spirit.

Since 2001, my journey has been filled with ups, downs, loopty loops, crash and burns, and miracles. In 2006, I almost lost the battle with depression - none of the coping techniques I had previously relied on were working, I spiraled uncontrollably. I was over-medicated and depended on the experts to heal me. I was chemically imbalanced, unable to focus or even care for myself for several months...my hair was falling out. I didn't recognize myself in the mirror anymore. I couldn't feel anything, physically or emotionally. I was beneath the bottom. I was dying inside and felt hopeless and after a suicide attempt I ended up in a mental facility.

I was so out of it, I couldn't participate in my own recovery. I would go to sessions and stare at the walls. Not even the promises of being granted a phone call to my son, or a visit from my brother or mom were enough to encourage me to try. I was ready to give up.

In one group session, I was listening to an older man tell his story, and I stood up and screamed. Everyone in the circle was shocked because I think it may have been the first time in days anyone had heard my voice. The therapist came and held my hand and looked me in the eye and said, "Scream again." I stared at her, but followed her directions and screamed and screamed and screamed until I was too exhausted to stand. She sat on the floor with me and said the most profound thing I had ever heard, "Tamika, you never wanted to die. You just wanted to stop living the way you were living."

She was right. I not only wanted to stop living the way I was living...my ability to live was literally dependent on having the courage and strength to find my authenticity. To define what being Tamika really meant to ME. Enter the foundation of this book.

Through the power of social media, family, friends, and followers have bared witness to me living life and somehow been inspired but more than any inspiration I gave them - they've inspired me! I've been empowered to live my life if not because it's literally why I am here, but also to be a light that guides others into embracing their ability to do the same. *LIVE! 5 Steps to Being More Free Spirited* is inspired by every person I've ever met that has said, "I wish I could be more like you." My answer has always rung with the same sentiment..."Do it...but aim higher...be more like YOU!"

Being free-spirited is a lifestyle, and just like any lifestyle change, it requires intention, dedication, and time to be effective. The goal is not to create a world of Tamika clones...(although now that I think about it....I kid, I kid)...but instead to bless this planet with the best in each individual who embarks upon this journey.

You deserve to be YOU. Unapologetically.Genuinely. Completely.

Before you turn the page, grab your journal, open your favorite note-keeping app, or even start a draft of an email to yourself (life-changing tip - create an email address where you can journal on the go and send messages from your main email there to yourself for safe-keeping, I have been doing this for years! I send voice notes, pics, messages I write to myself when my physical journal isn't available) - At the end of each chapter, there are some small assignments to help you focus on what this journey will look like for you.

Now, if you haven't tucked your tail to hide and run...let's do this!!!

CHAPTER 1

Define You for You

Tamika Lang
April 21, 2019

I've never claimed to be perfect.
Only that I'm the best Tamika L. (Anderson-Lee) Lang that I can be.
I'm not without flaws. I'm not without trials. I've not been the best daughter. My marriage has struggles. My children don't always embrace me.
But I own it all.
And I live my truth as best I can. I'm transparent because it keeps me humble.
I'm free-spirited because I deserve the world.
I give abruptly.
I cry silently.
I overcome daily.
I smile intentionally.
I love deliberately.
And daily I'm unapologetically my genuine self.

If you ask any adult who they are, they'll likely respond by saying things like:

- A mother/father
- A daughter/son
- A sister/brother
- A friend
- A/an (insert occupation)

Sadly we all get very caught up in identifying with our roles in life before we ever understand how to identify with being who we are! Isn't that crazy??? I mean we are literally taught in some capacity or another to be so many things and rarely is anyone taught or even encouraged to learn who they are outside of those titles and positions. Shit, even as I sit here attempting to explain this concept, it gets a little bit confusing because how can you define such an abstract thing???

You start with your best qualities. What sparks the fire in your soul? What gift do you have to share with the world? What is your purpose? What void do you fill?

See, what we don't spend enough time celebrating is the FACT that we are one of a kind. The very birth of each person on this planet was intentional and without even the shortest second of existence, nothing would be the same. We are all here to be impactful. How will you make your impact?

In 2001, I was 23 years old, a single mother, a student, working full-time, and managing several other responsibilities in my family but I really was unsure about what any of that meant. To this point in life, I was trying to achieve goals in life that weren't necessarily my goals, they were established based on expectations imposed by society. There's nothing wrong with using societal norms as a guide, after all, standards and examples have to come from somewhere... but for me... I felt like nothing was a good fit...I was unfulfilled and desperate to BE...So many of us go from being a child to a parent or to a spouse and never really have a second to just be ourselves...It's crazy that the one relationship we will literally have our entire lives is the one that is given the least amount of time to cultivate. The relationship you have with yourself should trump all others!!!

The world literally has the expectation of us to be everything for everyone that we have perceived obligations to before we pour into ourselves. This logic is what perpetuates mental illness. How can a house provide shelter if it has no walls and no roof? You have to build yourself.

So let's get back to the definition of you! Defining ourselves requires a level of honesty many of us are not comfortable with subjecting ourselves to. Defining yourself goes beyond the meaning of your name, your zodiac sign, your birth chart, your religious beliefs, your Hogwart house...lol. We are the sum total of all our parts. That means looking in the virtual mirror of your heart, mind, soul and spirit and honoring the greatest parts, and the deepest, darkest, most hideous parts too.

Listen...some of the most amazing truths are found in those deep, dark, ugly places. So take some time and leave no stone unturned as you define yourself. This requires a level of self-awareness and emotional maturity that most of us truly are not taught. But man, if you take the time to discover this, defining you for you will inevitably enable tapping into the material that is required to propel you to greatness. Then, get this...when you define you for you - that is the moment you will tap into the energy that is required to be free from the parameters set by outside forces and you will gain maximum control of your life and begin to move with confidence.

My deep dark parts are ugly as fuck! I own them. Sometimes too proudly...but what's great about defining you for you is that you're the only one that has to reconcile these bad parts...and the definition is evolutionary. You can get really comfortable with your total definition and stay there...but growth and change are inevitable so those identifiers will expand and contract and you may even eliminate parts and accept new ones...this is yours to create. I think one of the hardest parts about defining ourselves is understanding that we aren't stuck being who we were at one time or another. The "this is just the way I am" mentality is real and for some, it really may be their truth that they are ornery, evil, selfish, narcissistic, spoiled, or any host words with negative connotations that become crutches to self-discovery and cancer to relationships. And it really is ok to be accepting of those toxins and as ok as it is to never want to change - not wanting to change is not the same as being unable to change.

So take inventory of your character, desires, and what brings peace to your soul. When determining your definition the only mandatory stipulation is, to be honest. If you attempt to define yourself outside of your capacity you will be fraudulent and lose yourself or become imprisoned by the avatar you've created as opposed to operating in the freedom that exists in being the you that you were created to be.

When I began the journey to defining myself I started kind of like I start when I am trying to decide what I want to eat…lol. I started with the things I am NOT… I am not diabolical, I am not athletic, I am not soft-spoken, I am not shy, I am not great with emotions…etc. I never wrote any of this down, but I kept inventory.

I also stood literally naked in the mirror and told myself what was great about me. Tamika you are giving, you are a thinker, you are abstract, you are unconventional, you are fearless, you are peculiar, you are bold, you are pretty, you are sexy, you are hyper-intelligent, you are intense…and on and on…There's literally no limit to qualities you can accept as your definition. If you can't stand naked and love on yourself (yep, literally and figuratively) you can't begin this journey into the free-spirited life you deserve.

Journal time

"You may not have given yourself a name, but you can determine your own identity."

~Tamika Lang

What 5 things define you?

1. _____

2. _____

3. _____

4.

5.

CHAPTER 2

Care Less so You Can Do and Be More

Tamika Lang
December 23, 2020

One thing that set me free in life was realizing I don't owe anyone an explanation.

I may choose to graciously offer one with or without request...but no one on this planet is entitled to it just because we are in a relationship on some level whether it be family, friend, or other...

#Mermicornism

This chapter could probably be two words long, then the collection plate could be passed and the benediction pronounced...you ready? Here goes...

FUCK IT.

No, but really. Now that you have removed the pressure to be defined by anyone and anything else other than yourself...you're ready to denounce the holds and pressures that living by others' terms imposes. Now before anyone yells, "Fuck It," out the window. There are rules in the world, there are moral standards and I am by no means advocating law-breaking nor am I advocating disregarding humankind. What I am campaigning for is a mentality that the only opinion of you that matters is yours.

I know this is easier said than done. We live in a judgemental society. So many people have expectations of us. No one wants to be a failure, no one wants to disappoint the people they love, no one wants to be seen as crazy or seen in a negative light. But what if you could exist for 5 minutes in a world where you gave zero fucks about anyone else's opinion. Imagine the liberty that comes with this lifestyle. Well...I am here to tell you that you absolutely can exist in that reality. It won't be easy but it is absolutely possible.

There are two key components to understanding this aspect of the free-spirited lifestyle:

1. Understanding there is a fine line between being free-spirited and being selfish

2. Understand that opinions do not equal your truth.

Let's deal with the first point because it's the one that will keep you from feeling guilty as you navigate your freeness. Being a free spirit and living life on your own terms is not something that will be easily understood by the rest of the world. One reason why is because so many people are trapped in the prisons of their minds and will never relinquish themselves from tradition, stereotypes, and societal norms, in spite of their own dreams, desires, ambitions, and will.

The line between being free-spirited and being selfish is drawn when we lack the ability to be considerate. Being a free spirit and putting your needs first does not mean you disregard your family, friends, or responsibilities. It means understanding the difference between "No" and "Not right now." It means planning your adventures and planning for retirement can both be done. The moment you shit on anyone you love to get what you want you've crossed the line. Self-care is essential...Selfish moves will counteract your impact.

Achieving the balance is key, maintaining the balance is the goal. Falling short occasionally may occur, don't beat yourself up over it, just be intentional and committed to being balanced.

This brings us to the second component to caring less so you can do more. In addition to balance...you must remember the barometer for your balance is determined by you. Not by anyone's response to your actions or opinions of them. You have your own internal moral compass that will guide you towards peace or toward guilt.

It's perfectly ok to acknowledge others' opinions, feelings, and emotions surrounding your decisions and even to validate them. You can be respectful of the truth surrounding the perspective of those you care about without internalizing and accepting ownership of them as your own. You define yourself. You determine your truth. Some people will attempt to steal your light, joy, and zest for life out of the fear that they can't do the same, out of jealousy, out of ignorance and that's ok, whether it's intentional or not, it does not have to affect your choice to live the life you design.

I read a quote on a meme recently that said, "People pleasing isn't an expression of love, it's an expression of fear." If that stings...maybe you've been held captive in a life where you've lost sight of the balance between being a giver with a pure heart that gives for joy versus doing so because you don't want to lose the people you love. Maybe you give because you want something in return - be it love, admiration, or even to be compensated. Only you know your motives.

Determining your intentions while being aware of the intentions of those around you is wise. It's called discernment. Protecting your peace is paramount. That protection includes understanding what to keep and what to throw away.

There's an additional aspect to this Care Less/More essential, and that is removing the fear of being told no and/or being disappointed.

Being told "no" isn't a death sentence. It may not feel good or be your immediate desired response to a question but it's always an option. Removing the fear enables you to be able to prepare better to ask again or pivot and move on.

One of my favorite mantras is that you can either resist the wind and let it restrict your movements or you can lean into the wind and allow it to propel you to greatness. I'm not sure who said this but I adopted this concept many years ago while I was dealing with the principles of resistance vs avoidance. Fear is just a form of resistance, and resistance is a false notion that outside forces determine our movements.

Every second of every day we have choices to make. That very fact means we are constantly in control. Owning our power enables us to live in our freedom.

Journal time

"The only opinion of me that matters is mine."

~Tamika Lang

Name 5 opinions or societal norms/stereotypes that you need to disconnect from.

1. _____
   _____
   _____
   _____
   _____
   _____
   _____
   _____
   _____

2. _____
   _____
   _____
   _____
   _____
   _____
   _____
   _____
   _____

3. _____
   _____
   _____
   _____

4.

5.

CHAPTER 3

Remove Consequential Mentality

Tamika Lang
March 2, 2020

What if you condition your mind not to accept the possibility for anything other than the greatness of your purpose?

The sun isn't aware that darkness exists so it lives in a constant state of shining.
#Mermicornism

We are halfway there! And just like any journey when you get to the halfway point it's cool to look back and reflect. We covered two pretty difficult concepts and if you are still reading and not exhausted from the inventory you've done so far, pause and celebrate...because I'm not gonna lie...it's about getting a little tougher to make this lifestyle change. But listen, friend, I am here to guide you and make this as painlessly clear as possible.

Here we go...you read the title of this section and probably thought...What the hell does this even mean. Well, I am about to drop a bomb on you…ready...here goes…

There are no consequences in life. None. We all have a path and every step along our path is a part of the tapestry of our lives. Everything: great, good, indifferent, bad, worse, heartbreaking, and horrible are all essential. There are responses to actions that we must accept when we make choices but they are not designed to destroy us.

One of my favorite life philosophies is, "You're always exactly where you're supposed to be." We can weigh various outcomes based on our decisions but at the end of the day whatever choices we make there will be a result. Removing the mentality that it's a consequence releases us from the prison mentality that perpetuates anxiety, depression, fear, inadequacy, insecurity, and failure.

There are only two things that are absolute in life. One is that change is inevitable and the other is that death is eventual. Every given moment we are existing between change and on our way toward death. Sounds morbid but if you truly remove the concept that there are consequences and accept that we are all having human experiences that we are fully able to manifest you will realize how that opens the door to you being more free-spirited.

Let me simplify this...proof that consequential thinking will deter you from greatness is this...You have overcome 100% of the worst decisions you've ever made, survived, and thrived after 100% of the worst things life has presented you with. The pivotal moment may not have been instant and quite possibly was painful - but it was not permanent.

This concept is not meant to encourage carelessness but more so to promote courageousness. Have the courage to look silly, have the courage to try for the thrill of the experience.

We've been taught that we reap what we sow and we teach it as a means of explaining rewards and consequences. Even though...more often than not we speak it as justification for consequence...when in actuality it's a statement that supports the very real concept of results. Rewards are products of choices...they are the result of a choice.

Consequences (in the traditional sense), are products of choices...they are the result of a choice.

Some results may last longer, may affect greater change, but at the end of the day - good or excruciatingly horrible they are just results of a choice. A choice we are ALL free to make.

Changing the way you think and feel about choices will enable you to be less attached to consequential thinking.

Journal time

"Consequences do not exist. Every response to our choices is just a position on our path."

~TAMIKA LANG

Name 5 Choices You Might Have Made Differently, Were You Not Concerned with Perceived Consequences

1. _____

2. _____

3. _____

4.

5.

CHAPTER 4

Forgive

Tamika Lang
January 5, 2020

Let's talk forgiveness.

Alot of people have issues forgiving because they also think they have to forget. This is very untrue.

Memories are forever.
However, the energy and power you give them to control your emotions and peace of mind is directly tied to your ability to forgive.

Forgiveness says to your heart, mind and soul that you're reclaiming power and restoring energy to allow the 3 to obtain and live in peace.

#Mermicornism

What are you holding on to? Why are you holding on to it?

There is absolutely no way to be liberated if you are unable to forgive. Forgive others. Forgive yourself.

The first 3 chapters of this book were written in 3 days. My goal was to complete the whole project in one week so I could have it published the week after Thanksgiving. But life was life-ing and I chose to procrastinate a little. Leaning into the belief that we are always exactly where we are supposed to be…it wasn't by chance that I wasn't done…

2 mornings ago I woke up and was doing my usual social media stroll across IG, FB, and TikTok and heard the audio of a reel that said:

"Peace is the result of retraining your mind to process life as it is, rather than as you think it should be." ~Wayne Dyer

Man! That hit hard. I thought about it all day. It literally put me into a state of gratitude…befitting of this season we are in!

I had to retrain my brain. After MANY years of battling depression and anxiety, I realized that in spite of my belief that I had forgiven those who trespassed against me…I truly hadn't achieved the level of peace that accompanies sincere forgiveness.

Sincere forgiveness doesn't mean you forget the transgression. Our memories are gifts. Even the bad ones. What sincere forgiveness does is remove the power given to the trauma of the action. Forgiveness is essential for healing. Forgiveness is essential for freedom.

I like making lists...so when I made the commitment to living life authentically as Tamika, I made several lists. A few of them were things I needed to forgive...

It wasn't easy because like many people I had fallen into the trap of believing in closure...into believing I shouldn't or couldn't forgive without an apology. What a load of crap!!!

When I tell you this you may not believe me, but hey...it's my truth...the SECOND I understood that I am in control of my healing, that forgiveness is for ME! That, I can be intentional about releasing all that crap whether anyone ever apologized or not...I INSTANTLY felt lighter, relieved, and free!!! There were some folks that I reached out to and shared that I had forgiven them...and others that I haven't spoken to again to this day...that choice or necessity is yours to determine.

Tackling forgiving myself was a little more difficult. While I don't have an issue owning responsibility for my actions, I was having an issue understanding that forgiving myself didn't remove the possibility of my doing the thing that required forgiveness again or that I would even recognize that I was doing it... Plus, when you forgive other people you can stop fucking with them so they don't have the ability to do the thing again or do a new thing...but well...uh....you can't exactly remove your relationship with yourself.

Soooo...to forgive me, I had to be creative. I looked at my list, I looked at myself in the mirror and I simply said...Tamika, you made a choice. You survived the outcome of that choice. Let it go. Corny as it may be...it worked. It gave me the courage to say, Tamika, I forgive you for giving in to depression, for not believing I deserved happiness or peace, for not thinking I could determine my own identity and truth...and all the other things just started to flow until my soul was cleansed.

Journal Time

"Unforgiveness is like telling your spirit you like being in bondage."

~TAMIKA LANG

Name 5 People You Need To Forgive and List the Specific Transgression

Begin the statements with, "I forgive _____ for _____."

1. _____

_____

_____

_____

_____

_____

_____

_____

_____

_____

2. _____

_____

_____

_____

_____

_____

_____

_____

_____

_____

3. _____

_____

_____

4.

5.

Name 5 Things You Need To Forgive Yourself For:

1. _____

_____

_____

_____

_____

_____

_____

_____

_____

2. _____

_____

_____

_____

_____

_____

_____

_____

_____

3. _____

_____

_____

_____

_____

4.

5.

CHAPTER 5

Start and Stay the Course

Tamika Lang
October 8, 2019

They say the journey of a million miles begins with one step and I agree.

And while not all steps will be made confidently, successfully, or even supportively...the key to continuing taking steps is to remember the journey is yours to define.

Be bold...take a step.

#Mermicornism

Have you ever seen a runner bolt from the starting line at the sound of the gun, run five or six feet and sit down?

Have you ever seen one start on a track or course then decide they were better off on another track or course?

It's very likely that your answer is no unless you're an asshole and have to make this difficult...lol... Really the reason why is because you can't win if you don't start and stay the course.

Here's the thing...We all have a few things in common...We were born, we have 1 life to live, then we are going to die. The entire reason for your existence is linked to you being you...that means starting your life and staying the course.

If that sounds simple, it's because it is. Nowhere in any story of creation does it say being you is complicated. We make it complicated when we succumb to the beliefs that anyone or anything else can define us, determine our purpose or our happiness.

Everyone knows the feeling of accomplishing something. Whether it's remembering the first time you successfully tied your own shoes or rode a bike or when you graduated from high school or college...We all know that feeling. We focused on the task and let nothing stop us from seeing it through to the end. What if we too took that same approach in our approach to becoming the absolute best self we could be?

The absolute best way to truly rest in peace when we leave this world is to have lived a life with no regrets and to have left those we encountered better for having known us.

When I turned 41 I decided I was going to spend the year doing new things and having new experiences. That was the birth of "41 Firsts" and unbeknownst to me, the birth of "The Live First Movement." It was my goal to find new things each year from then on to challenge myself, to grow, to explore, to learn, to share, and more than anything to inspire.

Then the pandemic hit...talk about fucking up a plan! I was able to do a few firsts to get the 42 Firsts lists going, but I didn't complete 42 new things...that's when I (like everyone else) learned the value of pivoting. I also tested the truth in another of my favorite life mantras: "Those who remain flexible seldom get bent out of shape." Starting on a path and staying the course doesn't mean we have to be staunch and regimented...If we stopped every time life presented a challenge we would never accomplish anything. Those challenges just come along to force us to prove to ourselves just how bad we want it!!!

So tell me something…
How bad do you want your freedom?
How bad do you want peace of mind?
How bad do you want to be YOU? Unapologetically YOU? Wholly YOU?

What could possibly exist that would evoke a greater desire???

Journal Time

"When the pain of where you are becomes greater than the fear of where you want you be, your journey will begin."

~TAMIKA LANG

Name 5 things you tend to let get in the way or deter you from your goals:

1. _____

2. _____

3. _____

4.

5.

Name 5 things you can do to pivot, overcome, or conquer the distractions you are faced with:

1. _____

2. _____

3. _____

4.

5.

Name 5 things you have always wanted to do/see/or be

1. _____

2. _____

3. _____

4. _____

5. _____

Give the things above a deadline!

Start planning the celebration!!!

OUTRO

So I ain't no punk, but when I typed that last exclamation point, my ass cried real tears! This book might be small, but it's mighty and my prayer is that it inspires every soul that ingests it. If I can do anything on the planet...I hope it's to leave anyone that comes in contact with me better off for that encounter...

This book is just the beginning! The journal prompts are just the beginning! The real work begins when you read the last word of this conclusion and make the decision to put action behind the inspiration! Are you ready to live the life you've always desired? Are you ready to achieve the peace and destiny you deserve?

I'd love to share your journey with you! Whether it be through social media, as your Live First Coach, or as a guest on your podcast or motivational event!

For more information contact me at:
https://www.facebook.com/thelivefirstmovement
Or
https://www.instagram.com/thelivefirstmovement/

Also… be on the lookout for the next edition in the Live First Movement Series! "Redefining Forever." Coming Spring 2022!

Made in the USA
Columbia, SC
16 April 2025